STORM CHASERS

Sarah Tieck

ABDO
Publishing Company

VISIT US AT
www.abdopublishing.com

Published by ABDO Publishing Company, 8000 West 78th Street, Edina, Minnesota 55439.

Printed in the United States of America, North Mankato, Minnesota.
062011
092011

 PRINTED ON RECYCLED PAPER

Coordinating Series Editor: Rochelle Baltzer
Contributing Editors: Megan M. Gunderson, BreAnn Rumsch, Marcia Zappa
Graphic Design: Marcia Zappa
Cover Photograph: *photolibrary.com*: Oxford Scientific (OSF).
Interior Photographs/Illustrations: *AP Photo*: AP Photo (p. 27), Rick Bowmer (p. 17), NBC/NBCU Photo Bank
   via AP Images (p. 27), Andy Newman (p. 21), Steve Sisney/Daily Oklahoman (p. 15); *Getty Images*: YURI
   CORTEZ/AFP (p. 23), Hulton Archive (p. 25), Library of Congress/digital version by Science Faction (p. 25);
   iStockphoto: ©iStockphoto.com/sshepard (p. 21); *NOAA Photo Library*: Mr. Shane Lear, Orange Australia
   (p. 30), NOAA Central Library; OAR/ERL/National Severe Storms Laboratory (NSSL) (p. 13), Sean Waugh
   NOAA/NSSL (p. 13); *Photo Researchers, Inc.*: Mike Berger (p. 9), Jim Edds (p. 19); Jim Reed (pp. 5, 7, 9, 29);
   Photolibrary: Oxford Scientific (OSF) (p. 15); *Shutterstock*: DarkOne (p. 13), lafoto (p. 11), Daniel Padavona
   (p. 21), Varina and Jay Patel (p. 30); *US Air Force*: US Air Force photo/Staff Sgt. Michael B. Keller (p. 17).

Library of Congress Cataloging-in-Publication Data

Tieck, Sarah, 1976-
 Storm chasers / Sarah Tieck.
    p. cm. -- (Extreme jobs)
 ISBN 978-1-61783-028-0
 1. Meteorologists--Vocational guidance--Juvenile literature. 2. Severe storms--Juvenile literature. I. Title.
 QC869.5.T54 2012
 551.55--dc23
                          2011018117

CONTENTS

STORM CHASING 101

Weather events happen every day. **Meteorologists** study them. Meteorologists called storm chasers get up close to storms such as tornadoes and hurricanes.

Storm chasers risk their lives to learn about storms. The data they gather helps save lives. Now that's an extreme job!

Thunderstorms may last a few hours. Some produce tornadoes.

Hurricanes are large storms that can last for many days.

RIDERS ON THE STORM

When a storm forms, storm chasers get ready. It can take awhile for storms to strengthen. So, storm chasers may watch and wait for hours.

Storm chasers track a storm's path and strength. When the storm moves, they follow it.

Computers show a storm's path.

Storm chasers know a lot about weather. They study weather reports. And, they use special tools to measure outside conditions. Certain conditions form powerful storms.

Storm chasers are interested in the most extreme weather. They study how this weather causes storms to form, move, and grow. They find ways to get close to these storms while staying safe!

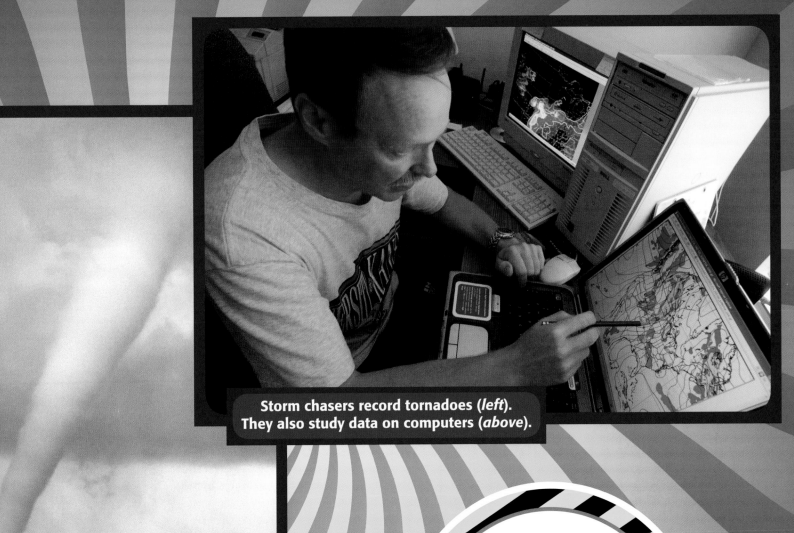

Storm chasers record tornadoes (*left*). They also study data on computers (*above*).

9

TOUCHDOWN!

Many storm chasers go into the field hoping to see tornadoes. But these spinning, twisting funnels of air can be hard to **predict**. And, they may last only a few minutes. During that time, some have winds faster than 300 miles (480 km) per hour!

Tornadoes form and move quickly. So, storm chasers move quickly to watch them.

Storm chasers work hard to be in the right place at the right time. They travel in cars, vans, or trucks to areas where storms are forming. Some days they may cover hundreds of miles!

Storm chasers spend at least part of the year working in the field. Most tornadoes form in spring or summer.

Many tornadoes form out of wall clouds. Wall clouds appear to hang low in the air.

The most powerful thunderstorms are called supercells. Tornadoes that form in these can cause much harm.

A tornado over water is called a waterspout.

FACT ALERT

In the United States, most tornadoes form in Tornado Alley. This area includes Texas, Oklahoma, Kansas, and Nebraska.

GEARING UP

In the field, storm chasers take notes. They note the sky's color. They measure the air **temperature** and the wind speed. They record the amount of rain or hail. And, they take pictures and videos of the storm.

Storm chasers have tools to help them track and measure storms. Computers and radios tell them what storms might do. Storm chasers also carry phones, maps, notebooks, and cameras.

Tornado pods are placed in a tornado's path to gather data. Scientists use the data to map and record what happens inside a tornado.

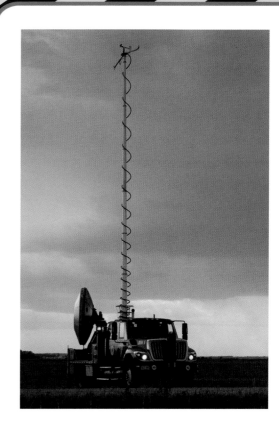

The Doppler on Wheels is a truck with a special radar dish on it. It maps storms.

Special storm-chasing vehicles help keep storm chasers safe from wind, flying objects, and hail.

HURRICANE HUNTERS

Other storm chasers study hurricanes. Hurricanes are powerful storms that form over warm seas. They can grow to be hundreds of miles across. If they hit land, winds and rain can destroy cities!

Airplanes take teams of hurricane hunters inside hurricanes. The teams measure the storm's direction and speed. They gather data they can't get from outside the storm.

Hurricane hunters fly through thick clouds!

Hurricane hunter planes are similar to other planes. All airplanes are made to handle strong winds.

Hurricane hunters fly to the storm's center, or eye. The trip can take ten hours or more! For most of that time, it is a smooth flight.

Hurricane hunters spend a short time in the strongest part of the storm. There, winds and rain shake the plane! Lightning may strike.

Hurricane hunters may pass through a storm more than once. This gives them a more complete record of it.

Hurricane hunters may drop special tools from the plane. The tools measure the storm and collect data.

FREE FALL CHUTE

19

WEATHER REPORT

There are often extra weather reports on television and radio during storms.

Storm chasers share data with other **meteorologists**, who give public warnings. Then, people in the storm's path know to take cover.

Storm watches mean storms are possible in the next few hours. Storm warnings mean storms are present or expected very soon.

FACT ALERT

In April 1974, more than 140 tornadoes occurred in the United States. Thirty of them were very powerful. These killed 330 people in 13 states!

SAFE SHELTER

When tornadoes happen, people take shelter indoors.

EVACUATION ROUTE

During a hurricane, people may need to leave their homes to stay safe.

READY, SET, GO!

Storm chasers are trained. They know how to **predict** weather and use weather tools. Most have a college **degree** in a science such as **meteorology**. Some have advanced degrees.

Weather balloons carry tools high in the air to measure weather. Students practice using them!

THEN TO NOW

One of the first people to study storms was Benjamin Franklin. Around 1752, he flew a kite in a storm. Lightning struck a wire tied to the kite. It went down the kite string to a key. The key sparked! This showed that lightning carries electricity.

In 1874, **naturalist** John Muir climbed a tree that was 100 feet (30 m) tall. He held on to the tree during a windstorm! In that way, he learned how weather affects trees.

Franklin's kite experiment changed ideas about science.

Muir explored nature. He became famous for helping create some of America's first national parks.

25

In 1965, David Hoadley started regularly following storms. Over time, others became interested in his work and ideas. So in 1977, Hoadley started a magazine called *Storm Track*.

In the 1990s, storm chasing became more popular. In 1996, a movie called *Twister* featured storm chasers. A television show called *Storm Chasers* started in 2007. It showed how extreme storm chasing could be!

⚠️ **FACT ALERT**

After storm chasing became popular, many people wanted to try it. But, it can be very unsafe. Storm chasers are trained to avoid danger.

Reed Timmer stars in *Storm Chasers* on the Discovery Channel.

In the movie *Twister*, actors Bill Paxton and Helen Hunt play storm chasers.

27

AFTER THE STORM

Thrills are just one part of a storm chaser's job. Many also do **research**. They study why storms form and what happens inside them. Pictures, videos, and other data may give them new answers. A storm chaser's extreme job can change science and save lives!

Storm chasers take pictures and videos of storms to study.

29

WHEN I GROW UP...

Explore parts of a storm chaser's job now!

Storm chasers predict when and where storms will happen. You can predict how far away a storm is by watching and listening. When you see lightning, count until you hear thunder. Every five seconds equals about one mile (1.6 km) away.

Storm chasers use maps and computers. Ask an adult to help you practice using these!

Storm chasers listen to weather reports on television and radio. What is the weather like where you live? Tune in to find out!

IMPORTANT WORDS

degree a title given by a college, university, or trade school to its students for completing their studies. An advanced degree, such as a master's or a doctorate, is earned by completing graduate school after college.

meteorologist (mee-tee-uh-RAH-luh-jihst) a person who studies weather. Meteorology is the study of weather.

naturalist a person who studies natural history.

predict to say something is going to happen before it does.

research careful study in order to learn facts about a subject.

temperature (TEHM-puhr-chur) the measured level of hot or cold.

WEB SITES

To learn more about storm chasers, visit ABDO Publishing Company online. Web sites about storm chasers are featured on our Book Links page. These links are routinely monitored and updated to provide the most current information available.

www.abdopublishing.com

INDEX